Images, Illusions, Hopes, and Fears

Contemplating My Life

By

Richard Edward Baker

Copyright 2015 by Richard Edward Baker

ISBN-13: 978-1519634801

ISBN-10: 1519634803

Dedicated
To

Mary, whom I love

and

All the people who have impacted my life —
For better or worse.

To those of you who loved me, you were right.
To those of you who hated me, you were right.
To those of you who only wondered,
this work is for you.

Table of Contents

Never Any Goodbyes .... pg 7
Thunder .... pg 8
Widows Walk .... pg 9
Pathways .... pg 10
Windows and Raindrops .... pg 11
Storm Song .... pg 12
Winter Leaves .... pg 13
The Pillars of Lagos .... pg 14
The Old Plow .... pg 15
Why? .... pg 16
The Thief .... pg 18
Night Passage .... pg 19
Shadows .... pg 20
Sighs of Angels .... pg 21
My Barefoot Woman .... pg 22
Soft Breezes Out of Africa .... pg 23
The Moorish Wall .... pg 24
Remind Me .... pg 25
Questions Answered Without Speaking .... pg 26
Maelstrom .... pg 27
Musicians in the Square .... pg 28
Fools Dance .... pg 29
My February Tree .... pg 30
Distant Dreams .... pg 31
The Mountain .... pg 32
Musings While Drinking .... pg 34
Legacy .... pg 35
It Comes on Cat's Feet .... pg 36
Love's Failure Departs .... pg 38
First Born .... pg 39
Deep Crimson Skies .... pg 40
Girl at the Bar .... pg 41
Evening Star .... pg 42
Echoes .... pg 43
The Choirboy .... pg 44
The Bearer of Darkness .... pg 46
Love's Oasis .... pg 47

Despair is a Black Bird ....pg 48
Angel's Question ....pg 49
Deafness of the Mind . ...pg 50

Never Any Goodbyes

I am part of the universe;
The universe is part of me.
Do not put me in some dark void.
Set my essence free.
Let me rise, coalesce with clouds,
And return to nourish or clean.
Scatter me in a place where
I quickly return to the earth and sea.
For what I believe is true:
Everything goes on and on;
There is nothing old or new.
I am part of you;
You are part of me.
Think of me for just a moment,
Now and then, and I am free;
And you and I have new hellos,
Never any goodbyes.

Thunder

Echoes of love, sounding like thunder,
Feeling like gentle rain,
Looking like gossamer clouds.
Passion rising, soft laugh to soothe the sighs.
Senses spiraling out to the universe,
Twinkling eyes promising heaven,
Shallow breathing, warm hands, fiery kisses.
Calm seas of joy splashing the beach where we lay.
The rapture of time spent in each other's arms
Tempered with the distance between us,
Magnified by our love, modified by our friendship,
Softly whispered good-byes, dreams of nights yet to be.

Widows Walk

The women in black pass my window,
Wearing the mantle of the widow.
Furtive glances from some;
Others fixing my reluctant gaze.
Silver locks remembered now,
With summer sun cascading brown
And gold against the morning haze,
Memories just behind their eyes:
Of youth and love, now only
Rekindled in an ageing reverie,
Yet new as their first embrace.
Of full layered skirts with bright patterns
To attract the young moths that
Danced about their flame.
So many years of caring
For their bright fliers now ended.
Pain and pleasure embraced and eluded;
Passion and youth now concluded.
The women in black pass my window.

Pathways

Pathways, meandering through the hills and valleys of time,
Sometimes clearly marked, unbending and sublime,
But always leading to that place, just ahead, beyond the rise,
Tomorrows and tomorrows, hasty farewells, missed good-byes.

The breakneck rush of youth, unmeasured distance run,
Now halts with sudden horror, we thought we'd just begun.
And now the destination clear, the pathway choices few,
I wish to pause and rest a while, and contemplate the view.

And by the roadside stands a sign, its message clear and true,
"Come here," it says, and I understand the message is from you.
So I'll wait here at this lovely place and shade my eyes to find,
You walking up the pathway that wanders through my mind.

And now you give me solace, wipe away the painful tears,
You take these tender moments and change them into years.
The tides will rise for eons, rushing headlong to the shore,
We lovers, having shared the kiss, will wish for nothing more.

Other lovers will pass this way and in these words delight,
Pause beside this lovely path and feel their souls ignite,
The mystery revealed to them, the one instead of two,
May hush their words and whisper soft homages to you.

Windows and Raindrops

Thunderheads roiling in,
Promising to cleanse the dusty windows of my eyes.
Bursting forth from their skyward abode,
They rush to earth, as if in some
Wind-driven dance,
Dashing themselves against the panes,
To relieve them of the dusty burden,
Placed there by the shifting sands of time.

As the storm rises,
The drops fling themselves to their task.
Some racing pell-mell from top to bottom,
In one wild race to reach their destiny.
Others, wanting to relish the journey,
Meander slowly, tangentially, but always
Inexorably toward their fate.
The brash ones, defying the gale,
Cling steadfastly to their place and,
Watching the storm depart,
Cry "Victory!" and sparkle in the sun.
Triumphant in their glory,
They do not feel the warming sun,
Slowly and imperceptibly bid them return,
Leaving the window as a mirror
Reflecting the blue sky,
Changed, yet the same.

And the raindrops, having left their kiss,
Rise to the heavens,
And, forming themselves into thunderheads,
Seek out the dusty windows of my mind.
And so it goes and so it goes....

Storm Song

It's 3:55. You're still asleep; I am watching you.
I am holding you with your back to me,
Smelling your hair, cupping your breast.
Yes, it sometimes rains at night, this time of year.
Lightning flashes over the sea, like fireworks.
The wind is picking up; it's blowing our curtains in;
They wave like the sea grass at high tide.
As the breeze drifts across your body, I smell Jasmine,
Honey, Sea Grass and salt air, mixed with your perfume,
The lovely fragrance of your body.

If there are gods, they must love us very much
To play their music for us.
Our souls are intertwined, the bodies follow.
With the sunrise, our storm song sung,
I will kiss your neck to wake you
And whisper praises of the sea.

Winter Leaves

A feeling, a glimpse of things usually unseen,
The soft echoing of hushed voices
In the cool, moist air of a dark, autumn night,
Wraps around the souls of ghosts yet to be.

Life flows in the veins,
And the precious gift is sent racing to that place
That holds the secrets of a life
Fired in the furnace of despair,
And quenched with the cool waters of another kind spirit.

What binds the soul to the heart?
Perhaps it is the subtle attraction of one love for another
That holds loneliness in check.
Standing on the edge of eternity listening to the soft rustling
around us,
Longing for the peace that awaits us in that darkness,
Yet loathe to leave the light behind.

It's only the sound of the dried winter leaves
that reminds us that time,
Unlike love, is finite.

The Pillars of Lagos

The Pillars of Lagos stand watch over the black sea,
Illuminated by the moon of time,
Keeping vigil for the sailors lost at sea,
Sons of Lagos, fishermen of fate, knowing the courage of self,
Yet seeking the reality of horizons yet unseen,
Prisoners to passions best felt in harbors yet to be discovered.

Ever watchful companions to the surf that created them,
Temporary guardians of the bluffs that hold their
replacements,
Mystical watchers, mirthful singers of the songs of the sea,
Knowing the secrets but holding them fast, locked in the stone
of heroes.

Men can never know the silent clock that ticks
With the seconds set by the Cosmos,
And played wave after steady wave,
Upon the shore of this lovely bay.
And in the pulsing throb of surf,
The music of the soldiers standing guard,
Faces turned to the sea which gave them Life,
Whisper softly, "Lagos, Lagos,"
And stare out to sea,
They look for me.

The Old Plow

It rests, a rust-red monument to itself,
Along the hedgerow near the field where
Many years of folding the earth
In soft furrows are now behind.

Labors left to younger workers,
Rewarded with kindness,
And placed there on the land it cared for,
Without style or grace.
'Tis a fitting place.

Why?

The Whispering Arch seems strange to me;
Some cold hand chiseled letters for all to see.
The message? "Work will make you free."
Oh, Noble Ones, no place to flee.

Your crime: the simple love of land.
What terrors wrought by man,
Parchment lies signed by bloody hands.
The Greasy Grass stained a crimson band.

Cold solace winter brings to thee,
Ancient frozen warrior of Wounded Knee.
Stifled screams, names we cannot speak,
Skeletal soldiers ride Sand Creek.

And still we drive you on and on;
No blood lust sated till you're gone.
Your lodges crushed, your murdered nation,
Our gift to you--the reservation.

Endless ghost riders through the Arch
Continuing the ceaseless march.
The wind whispers a wracking sigh;
It's single question, "Why?"

Still the maddening mob pursues,
Promised lands a madman's ruse.
Where beauty reigned as the fox,
Now children die from the blanket pox.

And yet you find the will to fight;
Cornered now, no room for flight.
Pursued by a devils greed for gold,
Kill the young; starve the old.

Tatanka's bones blot out the grass;
The hungry time has come to pass.
A mighty people, proud and tall,
Gray shadows for the famine's maul.

What soulless creatures, mouthing vespers,
Bring this holocaust with smiles and whispers?
Can no one see the price you pay,
And beg the headsman's axes stay?

Boxcars rattle to the boarding school;
War ponies replaced with plowman's mule.
And still you toil to keep the land
Of rocky earth and useless sand.

Oil becomes the reigning king,
And once again the hollow ring
Of broken promises and empty hands.
Murderers stalk your blackened lands.

You fight the white man's wars,
Raise his flag on foreign shores,
Smash the gates that horrors hold--
Treblinka, Dachau, Buchenwald.

The Ghettos and the Gulags close.
Were lessons learned do you suppose?
Dare we raise the warriors' chant
Of war crimes trials for Custer and Grant?

Will promises made remain only lies?
The ancient ones' songs, only death cries?
Or will history simply repeat and repeat?
Can the warrior clans accept this defeat?

The spirits still walk in the sacred places;
Cold warriors with painted faces
Still plead to the wind and the sky,
To answer one question, 'Why?"

The Thief

Softly slipping into my conscious reality,
Stealing into those precious hours of life,
Leaving in the wake of dreams a space,
Filled with confusion and dread,
Married in a cauldron of tortured thoughts a longing for the light,
Time is relentless in its pursuit of my life,
Always running just ahead,
And pretending to be lagging behind.

How do I capture this thief?
This robber of youth,
That strips the color from my hair,
And leaves sweet supple skin of birth a shrunken tattered memory
Of days spent rolling in the meadow of innocence.
Shall I grasp him by the flowing filaments trailing from the
promises of things to come,
And let him carry me away to a place of his choosing?

But no, he only holds the tattered rags of the past.
He can only hope for his existence in the future,
And I hold firmly to this moment,
As the warden of the thief.

Night Passage

Raging as the flood tide,
Surging breakers sweep the shore of restless dreams.
Memories and fantasies collide
In a relentless pursuit of wakefulness.
Sleep holds no respite,
Soothes not the haunted reality of scenes
Best left to hide in the darkened halls of time.

A light pulses in the fog of endless night
And brings solace to tortured musings.
The beacon beckons toward the safe harbor of a lover's arms.
Memories fade. Fears subside.
The sound of soft rhythmic breathing is the metronome
That heart songs are played in.
The ebb tide stillness brings the mind quietude, true sleep,
And a gentle passage on the ocean of the night.

Shadows

The shadows danced in Plato's cave.
We watched them for a while, you and I,
With soft smiles of understanding.
For we had discovered the sun,
And, having found it,
Returned to explain the light.
The figures continued the macabre dance,
Scorning us as fools.

So hand in hand, we left that place,
Out into the reality of the light,
For with all the pitfalls of the day,
It is better than the night.

We dance beneath the warming glow
Of the sun we have discovered,
Soft tears of joy for the love we have recovered.
The waltz plays on for us,
And we know the evening beckons,
But the darkness is a source of joy
For the sunrise follows.

You led me out into the sun,
Wrapped me in your light of love,
Sheltered my eyes,
Until they had recovered from the darkness,
Sang softly in my ear,
Until the echoes of the cave subsided.

These gifts are there
For all the souls that see our love and follow.

Sighs of Angels

You came to me as you traveled through space;
Your smile and laughter guided my soul.
Your voice, like the sighs of Angels.
Caring as a Shepherd watching his fold.

You bring me gifts yet unopened;
Your faith in me unbroken,
Marvelous as star-filled eyes,
Warming as a lover's sighs.

You share your thoughts and fears;
You wipe away my baseless tears.
Always when I think of you,
The sun comes pouring through.

A senseless man would wish for much;
I crave only for your touch.
The bell tower mocks my glance,
For time alone conducts the dance.

Come to me this little while,
And with your kindness make me smile,
For as our sands flow through the glass,
A love like ours will never pass.

My Barefoot Woman

She glides on unfettered feet.
The sunrise waits in purple skies,
Quiet passions, silent sighs.

I watch her come from out the sea,
Her glistening body, her breasts replete.
With outstretched arms she comes to me,
My barefoot woman comes lovingly.

I built this place near the sands,
She knows it well, the bed by the window.
She holds my face within her hands,
We trust this love, our hearts command.

And never more my love from thee,
Shall I wander on this earth.
Our hearts entwined, our spirits free,
My barefoot woman of the sea.

Soft Breezes out of Africa

Soft breezes from Africa, will soon brush your face,
Sent from the Atlas Mountains, humbled by your grace.
I see you seated there, at the café by the sea,
The overturned wine glass reserved for me.

How I envy the wind from the sea, touching you.
Gypsy guitars play through the night; love renews;
Starlight plays upon your face. Smile for me.
With closed eyes, passion ensues, and I can see.

You have taken my spirit where it longs to be,
Held my hand, caressed my vanity.
Walk with me a little while by the shore
And listen to the waves whisper, "I adore."

All those years ago, I sat with you,
Loving you, yet not knowing you.
Now sit with me once again, waiting for
Those soft breezes out of Africa, *mi amor*.

The Moorish Wall

No cold stone to us, "Home."
Fitted by some master hand,
We stand here as before
Beside the Moorish wall.
The centuries beckon us return.
Pounding drums of surf
Play ancient melodies at our feet.
Distant dreams repeat, "Home."
We are as spirits on the land,
Observed yet they cannot understand.
Through all the yesterdays revolving
Star-crossed lovers look to us enthralling,
Their pleas to us for solving.
We'll bring them home to the warm stones
And wrapping flowing cloaks around them
Hold them close unto eternity
And end the search on the sea of stars
To dwell with us at the Moorish wall.
And the Cosmos sighs, "Home."

Remind Me

Remind me when we return once again to the sea,
To remember the color of the ocean,
And commit to that special place in the hall of memory where
dreams are stored,
The temperature of the sand,
So that when the cold winter days return,
I may recall the wonder
Of these paradise days.

Remind me to record the sound of your laughter at my ineptitude
As a raiser of umbrellas against winds that wrenched it
From the place we had chosen to lay side by side,
And watched as it raced along the beach,
Until some kind stranger retrieved it,
And returned it.

Remind me to watch a little longer as you take your solitary walk
To those distant places in your mind.

Remind me to set the memory of your soft, well-oiled skin,
In my drawer of wide-awake dreams,
So that some night in a dark dream they will rescue the softness,
And hush my fears.

Remind me with that wonderful, soft voice that this gift,
Which we have wrenched from the hands of fate,
Is precious and only lasts for the moment,
Those little fractions of days that string themselves together,
Like an infinite rope of dream pearls,
And entwine themselves into the glorious hours we spend together.

Questions Answered Without Speaking

Our eyes met once, a furtive glance in a crowded room.
A simple question, asked and answered.
Just a touch of the hand, without contact.
A shared refrain, and soft tears of memories
Cloaked in the mist of time.
Realization of each other floods the conscious mind.
History repeats an invitation to the dance,
Asked and answered only with the eyes.

Questions answered without speaking.
Hearts racing with desire, dancing into the night.
We kiss till dawn, and the world is hushed to witness such love.
The ocean whispers to us, "Forever and forever,"
And weeps salty tears,
For never having known such passion.

And I gently caress your face,
And tell you of my love,
In the only way I know how,
With gentle tears and whispered words,
Softly murmured promises, yet to be kept.

Maelstrom

Drifting on the gentle swells of the Cosmic Ocean,
Spiraling in from the shores of the Universe,
Gathering up the fragments of memories,
Coalescing them into soft dream-filled cloud rafts,
Drawn eternally toward the center with such gentleness
That we are unaware of the maelstrom at the culmination of the
journey.

Love strikes with such a swift sure revelation.
The mind reels with the blow of awareness and,
Reaching out, catches the hand of the traveler
Sent by the mystics to guide each other.

The universe will continue its slow spiral
Toward the mysterious destination.
We will witness the birth and death of stars.
Galaxies, spinning off to their own destinies, will look back to us,
Envious of our firm position in the Cosmos,
Anchored by a love that defies the Maelstrom.

Musicians in the Square

Drawn as the moth to the flame,
I find myself carried to the sound of music,
In the stark white reflections of the square,
Illuminated by the sun as it can only be seen in the Algarve.
They sit as aberrations in black,
Each blending one to the other,
Clad in ebony from head to foot,
And yet making sounds that illuminate the souls
Of those wise enough to listen.

He, as if held by some magical puppeteer,
Breathes life into the silver flute in his fingers,
And it in turn attempts to fly free of his grasp,
But they are joined as surely as heaven and Earth,
In a dance seldom shared by lovers.
She sits at his side, gently caressing her guitar,
As the Madonna clasping the child to her breast,
Caresses the strings and causes the air to respond with soulful cries.
Children shout and laugh, the sound echoes from the surrounding walls.
Together they create a cacophony of sound that makes my senses soar.

Gifts bestowed to them; magic flows through them.
My heart is ignited with the love of sound;
Words flood the mind.
Each of us a poet in our own rite,
Prisoners to the gifts we have been given,
Laden with the love that drives us onward to perfect our sounds.
We are linked as shared souls, and condemned to our fates.
What sins we must have committed to have been given this burden;
What penance paid will grant us the silence of muted music,
And words that no longer sting the soul.

Fools Dance

The minute hand sweeps silently,
Inexorably, caressing our universe.
Stolen moments, love or curse,
Somewhere between passion and vanity.

Loneliness pervades the time, voids
The memories; promises condemn us,
Tightly sealed gifts held hostage,
But who pays the ransom wage?

Love practiced by fools, unknowing;
False passion, voiceless cock crowing.
Emotions, painted on faces, clowns;
Beauty, robbed of buoyancy, drowns.

False melodies, remind us by chance,
We are dancing the fools' dance,
And the minute hand sweeps silently,
Meter upon meter, mockingly.

My February Tree

(For Michele)

A tree grows in my garden, I planted it from seed.
It stayed there warm in the ground, all through the summer
And then it did the strangest thing:
It sprang to life one February day,
Impatient for spring,
Straining to reach the sun,
Not much more than a weed.

I nurtured it as best I could, protected it from the cold,
And marveled as it grew, despite the odds against it.
My little tree, really just a twig, always rushing to be big,
Growing as trees are want to do, upward and toward the sun.

There was always something to do in my garden,
But from time to time, I would just sit close by my February tree,
And marvel at the mystery of it.
Too small to offer shade, it spread its little branches,
And displayed leaves the world had never seen.
Even in my coldest months, they were always green.
As the years passed, my February tree rose straight and tall,
Always beckoning me near.
I basked in the beauty of the young green leaves,
And pondered what my tree would someday be.

Years roll by so quickly and so they have for me,
But always in my garden stands my February tree.
And now my garden basks in the shade of something splendid,
Blossoms of early spring bring sweetest fragrance to comfort me.
My garden still blooms, for how long we will see.
As the evening of the gardener beckons me to sleep,
The shade still lingers from my February tree.
The leaves whisper to me, telling me truths,
Keeping the chill winds of late autumn at bay.
When the last days of winter carry me away,
My garden will stand protected by my February Tree.

Distant Dreams

Distant dreams, languid hours beside the stream,
I have known you many times and many places.
In many guises, many faces.
I know your fear; I know your dream;
I am closer than I seem.

Wisps of memory, like gentle mist,
Recalls the passion in the kiss.
Mere mortals cannot understand,
The timeless touch of velvet hand,
That lingers till the stars disband.

So when the universe renews,
If lives again we are to choose,
Then I ask you, wait patiently,
For in the glow of things to be,
Find timeless love for you and me.

The Mountain

What is it about mountains that makes young men mad?

We see them across meadows of our youth and long to reach them;
We revel in the journey, making passing acquaintances with valleys,
Immerse ourselves in streams that cool our hot blood for a while,
But the mountains always beckon us onward.

The real question is which one do we climb?
Because the exuberance of youth tells us to climb them all,
We, as young men do, play in the foothills,
Knowing with misplaced certainty that we will know our mountain.
Do we select the mountain?
Or does the mountain select the climber?
Scenarios for old men to ponder.

How we love our mountain;
The climb begins with crunch of pine needles
And aspen leaves underfoot,
The sweet fragrance belying the gradually increasing slope.
But energy and optimism of sleek muscles and taut skin assures us
That we will conquer our mountain, and we eagerly press on.
At times, voices echoing from other peaks reach us.
We pause and listen for a while.
Most times we hear the lies of lesser climbers,
Claiming their mountain is where we should be,
And, recognizing them for what they are, climb ever higher.

I heard the beautiful sound of the Alpine horn,
Very softly beckoning me to the other mountain,
Recognized the beauty of the sound.
But I, as Odysseus bound by promises,
Turned a deaf ear to its beauty and climbed ever higher.,
After a while the soft, lovely sound receded,
Leaving only a dim memory of its beauty.

Now having spent so long in the climb,
The straps of the pack, stuffed to bursting
With unfulfilled wishes and dreams,
Cutting ever deeper into the shoulders of this aging climber,
Fingers bloodied by the sharp, cold stones of my mountain,
I hear from the resounding canyons at my feet
That low, beautiful sound of the Alpine horn
And recognize the player.
Too much time has been spent on my mountain;
The sound is beautiful but now so far away.
The cold white peak is as far away as when the climb began,
Now I realize it would have best been left to another man.
Mountains have a way of letting us be self-deceiving
And, wrongly chosen, lead to grieving.

Do I cling here on this rocky crag,
Or with abandon fling myself into the abyss
And, for as long as it takes to reach the ground,
Listen to the song now so well remembered
And, not with trepidation or alarm,
Welcome the warm green grass as it rushes upward to meet me?

What is it about mountains that makes old men mad?

Musings While Drinking

There's an echo in here, too many actors.
The stage is crowded, and the hall is ringing.
Heads down, searching for their marks,
Aware of the boards, but not the stage.
The play is cute, but the story is fractured.
The script is wordy, biting and stinging.
Who wrote this crap? "Author! Author!"
The roar of a one-handed ovation.
Here I sit, last row balcony, lousy seat,
Can't see a thing, but the tickets were free!
And just when you think it couldn't get worse,
There's a stirring in the orchestra pit--
Miracle stuff, this liquid I'm drinking,
The actors are sober; the audience stinking.
The music is awful, but it keeps me from thinking.
And now, my dear friends, if you will allow,
I will make my way stage center
And take my last bow.

Legacy

White walls reflect the glare;
Empty chairs, awaiting someone;
Unshuttered windows, vacant stare;
Empty tables, feasting undone.

Kindness, lost to fools;
Love, lost among the crowd;
Tenderness, ravaged by the rules;
Passion, beaten and cowed.

Life, passed off as living;
Lust, passed off as love;
Take, passed off as giving;
Hunters kill the doves.

Want has had its triumph;
Hunger starves the soul;
Weakness yearns for stronger stuff;
War exacts its toll.

And yet the children's laughter rings,
And young lovers sing the song.
Will history repeat the sting?
I pray that I am wrong.

It Comes on Cat's Feet

It comes on cat's feet,
Wrapped in a cloak as black as its abode,
Lying there patiently, just outside the door,
Purring lies.

I've known you before, Dark One,
Felt your soft breath on my cheek.
The light of life is the only illumination
For those cold green eyes.
Your sweet promises of peace belie the passage
That awaits the unwary and the weak.

But you and I are not strangers to the game.
I can speak my name. Not so you, lest you reveal
Your identity and, in doing so, diminish your appeal.

How many times have I seen the sadness you leave behind,
Caring not whom you take, like a street peddler,
Gathering the broken dreams and lives stacked along the curb,
Bargaining with their fear and vanity.

But this will not be the night I stroke your soft black coat,
Listening to that whisper that you conceal
With the velvet sound of angels' songs.
For love is only newly found,
And passion has a way of drowning out
Those dulcet tones you slyly use to sway.

So wait a while. For you the time is short.
You've wandered for Infinity,
And we've done this all before.
Remember, Dark One, life and love are not in your domain;
It's death that gives you privilege,
And I choose to remain.

But come again tomorrow night and listen at the door:
You'll hear no tears of sadness, no beating of the breast,
And when the earth is still, you'll curse the darkness,
And in the stillness find I've crept around behind you. . .
And now you hear an angel's voice, repeating in your ear,
That everything must someday end. . .
And even Death knows fear.

Love's Failure Departs

When it happens, do we know?
Or in the searching do we
Miss its passing, deadly slow?

Its blinding light we fail to see,
In its travel, lights no hearts,
And in the failure, departs.

Never lovers, more's the shame;
How I sought you, needing the touch,
But no passion given was requited such
That morning after brought such pain.

Strange the plans we make, agendas.
Foolishly I tried to hide rejection,
Once tasted still horrendous.
No new love rises without affection.

So as fault is parceled
My share is such that I loved unwisely,
And hoped that you would find love's fire.
Selfishly the touch withheld,
I could not find the pathway to.

Now the seeker admits defeat.
Tears shed for what might have been,
Flowing the furrowed face, much older and knowing,
Seeks a kinder journey, as twilight nears.

There is no fault in sunsets.
Still, with fewer left to find,
I pray you new beginning:
A good someone who will erase the pain
Of one who could not stay.

First Born
(For Richard, Jr.)

Maybe we can now speak of it,
The short hours we shared.
I wanted so much to take and guide you,
To try to hold out against time.
You filled me with joy and pride.
Little hands reaching for something.
Muted cries through the glass.
Separated only by space and yet,
I held you in my heart
From where they made me stand.
My brave son fighting for life,
And, in the end with a calm beauty,
We went to the place
Where I put you to bed for the last time.
Sleep well, my first born.

Deep Crimson Skies

Deep crimson skies.
The sea accepts the soft evening sun as a lover caresses the flesh,
Knowing but a fleeting passion,
Embracing the now setting sun as though for the last time,
But clinging to the hope of tomorrow.

The tide at flood calms the wind and stillness prevails.
Stars etch the skies with silver dreams.
Life holds its breath and waits the dawn.

Millenniums are but the ticks of a grander clock,
Set not by man nor aware of him.
Mountains rise, weather, fall, and are but beach sand,
Washed by the ocean of chance.
And the earth turns to meet the rising sun,
And the deep crimson skies once more.

Girl at the Bar

Hair, white as silver; heart, black as coal.
She waits for the offer that cost her the soul.
She caresses the toy bunny purse,
Remembers the first bedding,
When love was no curse.

Honeymoon nights without wedding;
Promises made and un-kept.
Now she holds strangers as lovers;
She stifles the tears to be wept
And smiles as she rolls in the covers.

In this place some give paradise kudos,
She knows not love, only lust.
The men only give their *escudos*,
And she knows better than trust.

The realities somehow avoid her,
And dreams of places now past
Seem only the realm of the voyeur.
Paid passion can never last.

So she sips the drink as if drifting
And thinks of a love long ago,
When trust was firm and un-shifting,
And thinks of a love long ago.

Evening Star

The evening star rises, above the horizon of my mind,
Shining with a brightness, that for love, is soft and kind.
Like mystics through the ages, we gaze and wonder why,
The universe chose darkness as the palette of the sky.

Scudding clouds embrace the moon in fleeting mist,
Silver glow descends, the earth is kissed,
She seeks the night in distant lands,
Moonbeams like the fingers of a lover's outstretched hands.

Rapture tiptoes like the Faun. Stars revolve; night is gone.
Soon purple skies pierce the night, a prelude to the dawn.
The Nightingale has sung the song, and stars have cast their glow.
The dawn comes forth with sunlit hair and warms the earth below.

The earth revolves, the day renewed, lovers rise,
Memories of dreams, moonlit dancers, quiet sighs.
Poets plead for words to show the essence of the night.
Lovers yearn for kindred hearts, and hope is always bright.

And now the sun regains the throne, not one to be outshone,
And dazzles gazers, daylight travelers, moving on alone.
We, the dwellers of the dark, await the night's surprises,
For sunset comes, and lovers stir whenever Venus rises.

Echoes

I stood at the rim of the canyon of life.
In my rage and despair I screamed,
"I hate you!"
My own voice, amplified, returned from the abyss,
Knocking me to the ground.

I whispered, "I love you,"
And voices from the lips of strangers,
Rising as a warm summer's kiss, flowed around me,
Bracing me against my cold emptiness,
Warmed my soul as if the corona of the sun were mine to share.

It does not matter where we stand on the rim of life,
It is only important that we care, and in caring,
We hear those soft whispers from the lips of strangers,
"Hold my hand. We stand together."

The Choirboy

Some are born to build a bridge;
Some born to tear it down.
Others can accomplish anything,
But only some are born to sing.

The voice, he was told, "a gift from God,"
By penguin-like figures, loathe to sing.
And when the little white boxes bring,
Cajoled the penguin,
"Sing boy, sing."

And so he did, with voice so clear,
Knowing the quiet children wrapped in white
Would hear his voice, as they passed into the light.
Sing boy, sing.

No tears are shed up in the loft;
Not knowing death his voice was soft.
The pleadings of the sobbing mothers ring,
"Sing boy, sing."

Voices reach the father, about this sickly son;
Who told him still a mystery, suffice that it was done.
False glory fills the chest, prideful demands sting,
"Sing boy, sing."

And now the strutting father, laying claim to the sound,
Makes the tour of relatives, round after round.
Children craving tenderness, what gifts they bring,
Sing boy, sing.

Does the monkey hate the organ grinder?
Or does he dance to make him kinder?
Maybe the chattering is the only reward it brings,
Sing boy, sing.

He tries to hold the anger, but the father goes too far,
And takes his singing monkey to his buddies in the bar.
He pounds the glass, for the attention it will bring,
"Sing boy, sing."

From somewhere deep inside him, the anger slowly wells.
There will be no Ave's on this night; false pride dispatched to hell.
The strident notes assailed the ears; the laughter level rising,
Sing boy, sing.

Gray coldness filled his eyes, as if the boy had told him lies.
Through the mocking crowd they moved, hollow laughter echoing.
A voice inside the boy approved the monster voice still lingering,
Sing boy, sing.

Forgiveness not a family trait, the father dies, still filled with hate.
The Choirboy stands mute for years; there were no gifts for giving.
The new son came into the world, and joy is for the living,
Sing boy, sing.

The little son is snatched away; the gods are vengeful bastards.
Is it just the price we pay, when sons betray their masters?
No! this cannot be the case, for songs of love still spring,
Sing boy, sing.

For somewhere in the future lies renewal of those loving ties,
And with the son whose stay was brief, The Choirboy will realize,
What's lost has now been found. And *acappella* voices ring,
Sing boys, sing!

The Bearer of Darkness

Stand behind me and I shall protect you
From the forces arrayed against me.
I guard my bastions religiously,
Against those who would drag me into the light.
My fear will hold out the Demon Truth:
I will not let it harm you.

You need only kneel at the altar, built with the bones and ashes
I have gathered together over the long centuries I have survived.
I will set a feast before you.
You will be fed and nurtured by those who call me Savior.
Fear not the winds of Reason,
For I have sealed the doors with my strongest warriors,
Hate and Stupidity, which have always held them out.

My windows are draped with tapestries,
Painstakingly embroidered in shimmering threads of fool's gold,
Using the dulled needle of arrogant gods
To emblazon half-truths and outright lies on my Coat of Arms,
A rampant Ogre sowing the seeds of hate on a field of ignorance.

The light of Compassion will not blind you to my truths.
Silence will be my bequest to those who know me and do nothing.
My wars will leave the smell of death
To replace the stench of Indifference.
The pink flesh of your children will be sacrificed
In the defense of my distorted text.

Golgotha is my garden,
For my name is Intolerance,
The Bearer of Darkness.

Love's Oasis

How does one separate life and love?
They can exist one without the other,
But they atrophy and die quickly without each other.
Shall we deny love to life? We can, but at what cost?
Life is not so precious as to hold love in abeyance.
When we open ourselves to love, we grow.
Without love, life is frozen fire, beautiful but pointless.
Wanderers in the void of loneliness find shelter.
The discovery of a loving heart brings realization
To fools who have worshipped at the altar of lust.
The touch of a gentle hand soothes the scarred soul.
Ecstasy is found in the whispered word of a kindred spirit.
Soft kisses prevail as passion subsides, and bids it return,
And the tree of life blossoms at love's oasis.

Despair Is a Black Bird

Like a great black bird with a broken wing,
This dark thing crawls over a life,
Smothering the light, making good seem evil,
Sucking the essence of the light,
Mindlessly shrieking parables,
And having no useable answers to our plight,
Mocking our futile attempts at kindness and soft words of longing,
Knowing the emptiness.

The tolling of a fractured bell drowns a shallow voice.
Clinging to the void of a life spent not in living,
But playing the role of jester,
Conjuring up fantasies.
Creating a world of make-believe
To hide the cruel fact of man's ability
To produce more hate than love,
Sustained by a school of ignorance,
Staffed by teachers of compliance,
Attended by fools.

And the great black bird consumes the carrion of unrequited love,
And conjures the feast which,
Presented at the table of despair,
Appeases its hunger.

Angel's Question

When the spring comes and the flowers bloom,
You will see my face.
When the soft breeze brushes your hair,
You will hear my voice.

When summer comes and the sun is high,
You will know my passion
As it warms your life.

When autumn comes, as we know it will,
And the trees reach golden fingers to the skies,
You will see your reflection in my eyes.

When winter comes, all cold and white,
You will feel my arms enfold you
As I repeat the promises I once told you.

And when time has come, if the gods are true,
When time itself will not renew,
I will walk among the stars . . . with you.

Deafness of the Mind

Staring into the white void, helpless;
A deafness of the mind, hopeless;
All the word music silent, oppressive;
The need to write remains obsessive.

Is there a gift or merely desire?
The mind burns with a fire.
A lance driven through the soul is kind,
And preferable to a barren mind.

Fleeting phrases like wisps of wind evade
The touch, like whores that first must be paid.
But what price is now demanded
For the words we once commanded?

Vincent, I understand the Starry Night,
Garish moonbeams, the muted fright;
And if the words abandon me,
Then I, like you, shall flee

Into that eternal darkness hence;
Break the pens that vex the sense.
Drifting through the cosmic fires,
An apt reward for poetic liars.

Word pictures may yet abound,
And sunlit fields of sound
May entice the soul to stay,
And search for words one more day.

But for the soul, the words hold danger
Of exposure to the total stranger.
Do I hide the words so witless fools
Find nothing but to ridicule?

Or is it the safety of blank page glowing,
That truly keeps the world from knowing
One poor poet's right to flee:
Do I hide the words to hide from me?

Made in the USA
Middletown, DE
28 March 2020